The Definitive Dash Diet Plan

Super Easy and Super tasty Dishes to enjoy in the best way Possible your everyday meals

Natalie Puckett

Table of Contents

Easy Garlic Almond Butter Shrimp

Serving: 4

Prep Time: 15 minutes

Cook Time: 30 minutes

Ingredients:

pounds shrimp

1-2 tablespoons garlic, minced

½ cup almond butter

1 tablespoon lemon pepper seasoning

½ teaspoon garlic powder

How To:

1. Pre-heat your oven to 300 degrees F.
2. Take a bowl and mix in garlic and almond butter.
3. Place shrimp in a pan and dot with almond butter garlic mix.
4. Sprinkle garlic powder and lemon pepper.
5. Bake for 30 minutes.

6. Enjoy!

Nutrition (Per Serving)

Calories: 749

Fat: 30g

Net Carbohydrates: 7g

Protein: 74g

Blackened Tilapia

Serving: 2

Prep Time: 9 minutes

Cook Time: 9 minutes

Ingredients:

1 cup cauliflower, chopped

1 teaspoon red pepper flakes

1 tablespoon Italian seasoning

1 tablespoon garlic, minced

ounces tilapia

cup English cucumber, chopped with peel

tablespoons olive oil

1 sprig dill, chopped

1 teaspoon stevia

tablespoons lime juice

2 tablespoons Cajun blackened seasoning

How To:

1. Take a bowl and add the seasoning ingredients (except Cajun).

2. Add a tablespoon of oil and whip.

3. Pour dressing over cauliflower and cucumber.

4. Brush the fish with olive oil on both sides.

5. Take a skillet and grease it well with 1 tablespoon of olive oil.

6. Press Cajun seasoning on both sides of fish.

7. Cook fish for 3 minutes per side.

8. Serve with vegetables and enjoy!

Nutrition (Per Serving)

Calories: 530

Fat: 33g

Net Carbohydrates: 4g

Protein: 32g

Light Lobster Bisque

Serving: 4

Prep Time: 10 minutes 400

Cook Time: 6 minutes

Ingredients:

1 cup diced carrots

1 cup diced celery

29 ounces diced tomatoes

2 minced whole shallots 1 clove of minced garlic

1 tablespoon butter

32-ounce chicken broth, low-sodium

1 teaspoon dill, dried

1 teaspoon freshly ground black pepper

½ teaspoon paprika

lobster tails

1-pint heavy whipping cream

How To:

1. Add butter, garlic and minced shallots to a microwave safe bowl.

2. Microwave for 2-3 minutes on HIGH.

3. Add tomatoes, celery, carrot, minced shallots, garlic to your Instant Pot.

4. Add chicken broth and spices to the Pot.

5. Use a knife to cut the lobster tails if you prefer and add them to the Instant Pot.

6. Lock the lid and cook on HIGH pressure for 4 minutes.

7. Release the pressure naturally over 10 minutes.

8. Use an immersion blender to puree to your desired chunkiness.

9. Serve and enjoy!

Nutrition (Per Serving)

Calories: 437

Fats: 17g

Carbs: 21g

Protein: 38g

Herbal Shrimp Risotto

Serving: 4

Prep Time: 10 minutes

Cook Time: 8 minutes

Ingredients:

2 pounds shrimp with their tails removed

cup instant rice

cups vegetable broth

1 chopped up onion

1 cup chicken breast cut into fine strips ¼ cup lemon juice

1 teaspoon crushed red pepper

¼ cup parsley

¼ cup fresh dill

pieces chopped up garlic cloves

1 tablespoon black pepper

½ cup parmesan

1 cup mozzarella cheese

How To:

1. Add the listed ingredients to your Instant Pot and stir.
2. Lock the lid and cook on HIGH pressure for 8 minutes.
3. Release the pressure naturally over 10 minutes.
4. Open lid and top with cheese.
5. Serve hot and enjoy!

Nutrition (Per Serving)

Calories: 463

Fat: 8g

Carbohydrates: 63g

Protein: 29g

Thai Pumpkin Seafood Stew

Serving: 4

Prep Time: 5 minutes

Cook Time: 35 minutes

Ingredients:

1 ½ tablespoons fresh galangal, chopped

1 teaspoon lime zest

1 small kabocha squash

32 medium sized mussels, fresh

1 pound shrimp

16 thai leaves

1 can coconut milk

1 tablespoon lemongrass, minced

garlic cloves, roughly chopped

32 medium clams, fresh

½ pounds fresh salmon

tablespoons coconut oil

Pepper to taste

How To:

1. Add coconut milk, lemongrass, galangal, garlic, lime leaves in a small-sized saucepan, bring to a boil.

2. Let it simmer for 25 minutes.

3. Strain mixture through a fine sieve into the large soup pot and bring to a simmer.

4. Add oil to a pan and heat up, add Kabocha squash.

5. Season with salt and pepper, sauté for 5 minutes.

6. Add mix to coconut mix.

7. Heat oil in a pan and add fish shrimp, season with salt and pepper, cook for 4 minutes.

8. Add mixture to coconut milk, mix alongside clams and mussels.

9. Simmer for 8 minutes, garnish with basil and enjoy!

Nutrition (Per Serving)

Calories: 370

Fat: 16g

Net Carbohydrates: 10g

Protein: 16g

Pistachio Sole Fish

Serving: 4

Prep Time: 5 minutes

Cook Time: 10 minutes

Ingredients:

(5 ounces) boneless sole fillets

Sunflower seeds and pepper as needed

½ cup pistachios, finely chopped

Juice of 1 lemon

1 teaspoon extra virgin olive oil

How To:

1. Pre-heat your oven to 350 degrees F.

2. Line a baking sheet with parchment paper and keep it on the side.

3. Pat fish dry with kitchen towels and lightly season with sunflower seeds and pepper.

4. Take a small bowl and stir in pistachios.

5. Place sole on the prepared baking sheet and press 2 tablespoons of pistachio mixture on top of each fillet.

6. Drizzle fish with lemon juice and olive oil.

7. Bake for 10 minutes until the top is golden and fish flakes with a fork.

8. Serve and enjoy!

Nutrition (Per Serving)

Calories: 166

Fat: 6g

Carbohydrates: 2g

Protein: 26g

Garlic Cottage Cheese Crispy

Serving: 4

Prep Time: 5 minutes

Cook Time: 2 minutes

Ingredients:

1 cup cottage cheese

½ teaspoon Garlic powder

Pinch of pepper

Pinch of onion powder

How To:

1. Take a skillet and place it over medium heat.
2. Take a bowl and mix in cheese and spices.
3. Scoop half a teaspoon of the cheese mix and place in the pan.
4. Cook for 1 minute per side.
5. Repeat until done.
6. Enjoy!

Nutrition (Per Serving)

Calories: 70

Fat: 6g

Carbohydrates: 1g

Protein: 6g

Tasty Cucumber Bites

Serving: 4

Prep Time: 5 minutes

Cook Time: nil

Ingredients:

1 (8 ounce) cream cheese container, low fat

1 tablespoon bell pepper, diced

1 tablespoon shallots, diced

1 tablespoon parsley, chopped

2 cucumbers

Pepper to taste

How To:

1. Take a bowl and add cream cheese, onion, pepper, parsley.
2. Peel cucumbers and cut in half.
3. Remove seeds and stuff with cheese mix.
4. Cut into bite sized portions and enjoy!

Nutrition (Per Serving)

Calories: 85

Fat: 4g

Carbohydrates: 2g

Protein: 3g

Juicy Simple Lemon Fat Bombs

Serving: 3

Prep Time: 10 minutes

Cooking Time: / Freeze Time: 2 hours

Ingredients:

1 whole lemon

4 ounces cream cheese

2 ounces butter

2 teaspoons natural sweetener

How To:

1. Take a fine grater and zest your lemon.
2. Squeeze lemon juice into a bowl alongside the zest.
3. Add butter, cream cheese to a bowl and add zest, salt, sweetener and juice.
4. Stir well using a hand mixer until smooth.
5. Spoon mix into molds and freeze for 2 hours.
6. Serve and enjoy!

Nutrition (Per Serving)

Total Carbs: 4g

Fiber: 1g

Protein: 4g

Fat: 43g

Calories: 404

Chocolate Coconut Bombs

Serving: 12

Prep Time: 20 minutes

Cooking Time: None

Freeze Time: 1 hour

Ingredients:

½ cup dark cocoa powder

½ tablespoon vanilla extract

5 drops stevia

1 cup coconut oil, solid

tablespoon peppermint extract

How To:

1. Take a high-speed food processor and add all the ingredients.

2. Blend until combined.

3. Take a teaspoon and drop a spoonful onto parchment paper.

4. Refrigerate until solidified and keep refrigerated.

Nutrition (Per Serving)

Total Carbs: 0g

Fiber: 0g

Protein: 0g

Fat: 14g

Calories: 126

Terrific Jalapeno Bacon Bombs

Serving: 2

Prep Time: 15 minutes

Cook Time: 10 minutes

Ingredients:

12 large jalapeno peppers

16 bacon strips

6 ounces full fat cream cheese

2 teaspoon garlic powder

1 teaspoon chili powder

Iow To:

. Pre-heat your oven to 350 degrees F.

:. Place a wire rack over a roasting pan and keep it on the ide.

. Make a slit lengthways across jalapeno pepper and scrape ut the seeds, discard them.

. Place a nonstick skillet over high heat and add half of our bacon strips, cook until crispy.

5. Drain them.

6. Chop the cooked bacon strips and transfer to large bowl.

7. Add cream cheese and mix.

8. Season the cream cheese and bacon mix with garlic and chili powder.

9. Mix well.

10. Stuff the mix into the jalapeno peppers with and wrap a raw bacon strip all around.

11. Arrange the stuffed wrapped jalapeno on prepared wire rack.

12. Roast for 10 minutes.

13. Transfer to cooling rack and serve!

Nutrition (Per Serving)

Calories: 209

Fat: 9g

Net Carbohydrates: 15g

Protein: 9g

Yummy Espresso Fat Bombs

Serving: 24

Prep Time: 20 minutes

Cooking Time: nil Freeze Time: 4 hours

Ingredients:

5 tablespoons butter, tender

3 ounces cream cheese, soft

2 ounces espresso

4 tablespoons coconut oil

2 tablespoons coconut whipping cream

2 tablespoons stevia

How To:

1. Prepare your double boiler and melt all ingredients (except stevia) for 3-4 minutes and mix.

2. Add sweetener and mix using hand mixer.

3. Spoon mixture into silicone muffin molds and freeze for 4 hours.

4. Remove fat bombs and enjoy!

Nutrition (Per Serving)

Total Carbs: 1.3g

Fiber: 0.2g

Protein: 0.3g

Fat: 7g

Crispy Coconut Bombs

Serving: 6

Prep Time: 10 minutes

Cooking Time: / Freeze Time: 1-2 hours

Ingredients:

14 ½ ounces coconut milk

¾ cup coconut oil

1 cup unsweetened coconut flakes

20 drops stevia

How To:

1. Microwave your coconut oil for 20 seconds in microwave.
2. Mix in coconut milk and stevia in the hot oil.
3. Stir in coconut flakes and pour the mixture into molds.
4. Let it chill for 60 minutes in fridge.
5. Serve and enjoy!

Nutrition (Per Serving)

Total Carbs: 2g

Fiber: 0.5g

Protein: 1g

Fat: 13g

Calories: 123

Net Carbs: 1g

The Sweet Potato Acid Buster

Serving: 2

Prep Time: 5 minutes

Ingredients:

1 cup sweet potato, chopped

1 cup almond milk

¼ teaspoon nutmeg

¼ teaspoon ground cinnamon

1 teaspoon flaxseed

1 small avocado, cubed

Few spinach leaves, torn

Toppings:

Handful of crushed almonds

Handful of crushed cashews

3 tablespoons orange juice

How To:

1. Blend all the ingredients until smooth.
2. Add a few ice cubes to make it chilled.
3. Add your desired toppings.
4. Enjoy!

Nutrition (Per Serving)

Calories: 200

Fat: 10g

Carbohydrates: 14g

Protein 2g

The Sunshine Offering

Serving: 2

Prep Time: 5 minutes

Ingredients:

2 cups fresh spinach

1 ½ cups almond milk ½ cup coconut water

3 cups fresh pineapple

2 tablespoons coconut unsweetened flakes

How To:

1. Add all the listed ingredients to your blender.
2. Blend until smooth.
3. Add a few ice cubes and serve the smoothie.
4. Enjoy!

Nutrition (Per Serving)

Calories: 200

Fat: 10g

Carbohydrates: 14g

Protein 2g

The Sleepy Bug Smoothie

Serving: 2

Prep Time: 5 minutes

Ingredients:

1 cup fennel tea infusion

1 cup almond milk

1 cup watermelon, chopped

1 green apple

½ cup pomegranate

½ inch ginger

Stevia to sweeten

How To:

1. Add the listed ingredients to your blender.
2. Blend until smooth.
3. Add a bit of stevia if you want more sweetness.
4. Serve chilled and enjoy!

Nutrition (Per Serving)

Calories: 200

Fat: 10g

Carbohydrates: 14g

Protein 2g

Matcha Coconut Smoothie

Serving: 2

Prep Time: 5 minutes

Cook Time: Nil

Ingredients:

1 whole banana, cubed

1 cup frozen mango, chunked

2 kale leaves, torn

3 tablespoons white beans

2 tablespoons shredded coconut

½ teaspoon Matcha green tea powder

1 cup water

How To:

1. Add banana, kale, mango, white beans, Matcha powder and white beans to the blender.
2. Blend until you have a nice smoothie.
3. Serve and enjoy!

Nutrition (Per Serving)

Calories: 200

Fat: 10g

Carbohydrates: 14g

Protein 2g

Ravishing Apple and Cucumber Glass

Serving: 2

Prep Time: 5 minutes

Ingredients:

1 green apple

2 cucumbers, peeled

1 cup almond milk

½ cup coconut cream (raw and organic) Pinch of cinnamon and nutmeg (each) Pinch of Himalayan salt 1 tablespoon coconut oil

How To:

1. Add all the listed ingredients to your blender (except oil, spices and salt).
2. Blend until smooth.
3. Mix in coconut oil, spices and salt.
4. Stir and enjoy!

Nutrition (Per Serving)

Calories: 200

Fat: 10

Carbohydrates: 14g

Protein 2g

Creative Winter Smoothie

Serving: 2

Prep Time: 5 minutes

Ingredients:

3 tomatoes, peeled

1 celery stalk

2 cloves garlic, peeled

1-inch ginger, peeled

1 cucumber, peeled

Juice of 1 lemon

1 cup alkaline water

Salt as needed

Pepper as needed

Pinch of turmeric

Olive oil/avocado oil

How To:

1. Add tomatoes, celery, garlic, cucumber and water to your blender.

2. Blend well until smooth.

3. Add lemon juice, salt and oil.

4. Stir.

5. Season with pepper and turmeric.

6. Stir.

7. Serve chilled and enjoy!

Nutrition (Per Serving)

Calories: 200

Fat: 10g

Carbohydrates: 14g

Protein 2g

The Hearty Garlic and Mushroom Crunch

Serving: 6

Prep Time: 10 minutes

Cooking Time: 8 hours

Ingredients:

¼ cup vegetable stock

2 tablespoons extra virgin olive oil

1 tablespoon Dijon mustard

1 teaspoon dried thyme

1 teaspoon sea salt

½ teaspoon dried rosemary

¼ teaspoon fresh ground black pepper

2 pounds cremini mushrooms, cleaned

6 garlic cloves, minced

¼ cup fresh parsley, chopped

How To:

1. Take a small bowl and whisk in vegetable stock, mustard, olive oil, salt, thyme, pepper and rosemary.

2. Add mushrooms, garlic and stock mix to your Slow Cooker.

3. Close lid and cook on LOW for 8 hours.

4. Open lid and stir in parsley.

5. Serve and enjoy!

Nutrition (Per Serving)

Calories: 92

Fat: 5g

Carbohydrates: 8g

Protein: 4g

Easy Pepper Jack Cauliflower

Serving: 6

Prep Time: 10 minutes

Cooking Time: 3 hours 35 minutes

Ingredients:

1 head cauliflower

¼ cup whipping cream 4 ounces cream cheese

½ teaspoon pepper

1 teaspoon salt

2 tablespoons butter

4 ounces pepper jack cheese

How To:

1. Grease slow cooker and add listed ingredients.
2. Stir and place lid, cook on LOW for 3 hours.
3. Remove lid and add cheese, stir.
4. Place lid and cook for 1 hour more.
5. Enjoy!

Nutrition (Per Serving)

Calories: 272

Fat: 21g

Carbohydrates: 5g

Protein: 10g

The Brussels Platter

Serving: 4

Prep Time: 15 minutes

Cooking Time: 4 hours

Ingredients:

1 pound Brussels sprouts, bottoms trimmed and cut

1 tablespoon olive oil

1 ½ tablespoons Dijon mustard

Salt and pepper to taste

½ teaspoon dried tarragon

How To:

1. Add Brussels sprouts, mustard, water, salt and pepper to your Slow Cooker

2. Add dried tarragon. 3. Stir well and cover.

3. Cook on LOW for 5 hours, making sure to keep cooking until the Brussels sprouts are tender.

4. Stir well and arrange.

5. Add Dijon over the Brussels sprouts.

6. Enjoy!

Nutrition (Per Serving)

Calories: 83

Fat: 4g

Carbohydrates: 11g

Protein: 4g

The Crazy Southern Salad

Serving: 2

Prep Time: 10 minutes

Cook Time: nil

Ingredients:

5 cups Romaine lettuce

½ cup sprouted black beans

1 cup cherry tomatoes, halved

1 avocado, diced

¼ cup almonds, chopped

½ cup of fresh cilantro

½ cup of Salsa Fresca

How To:

1. Take a large sized bowl and add lettuce, tomatoes, beans, almonds, cilantro, avocado, Salsa Fresco
2. Toss everything well and mix them
3. Divide the salad into serving bowls and serve!

4. Enjoy!

Nutrition (Per Serving)

Calories: 211

Fat: 16g

Carbohydrates: 6g

Protein: 10g

Kale and Carrot with Tahini Dressing

Serving: 1

Prep Time: 15 minutes

Cook Time: nil

Ingredients:

Handful of kale

1 tablespoon tahnini

½ head lettuce

Pinch of garlic powder

1 tablespoon olive oil

Juice of ½ lime

1 carrot, grated

How To:

1. Add kale and roughly chopped lettuce to a bowl.
2. Add grated carrots to the greens and mix.

3. Take a small bowl and add the remaining ingredients, mix well.

4. Pour dressing on top of greens and toss.

5. Enjoy!

Nutrition (Per Serving)

Calories: 249

Fat: 11g

Carbohydrates: 35g

Protein: 10g

Crispy Kale

Serving: 4

Prep Time: 10 minutes

Cook Time: 25 minutes

Ingredients:

3 cups kale, stemmed and thoroughly washed, torn in 2-inch pieces

1 tablespoon extra-virgin olive oil

½ teaspoon chili powder

¼ teaspoon sea salt

How To:

1. Prepare your oven by pre-heating to 300 degrees F.
2. Line 2 baking sheets with parchment paper and keep them on the side.
3. Dry kale and transfer to a large bowl.
4. Add olive oil and toss, making sure to cover the leaves well.

5. Season kale with salt, chili powder and toss.

6. Divide kale between baking sheets and spread into single layer.

7. Bake for 25 minutes until crispy.

8. Let them cool for 5 minutes, serve.

9. Enjoy!

Nutrition (Per Serving)

Calories: 56

Fat: 4g

Carbohydrates: 5g

Protein: 2g

Fancy Banana Oatmeal

Serving: 4

Prep Time: 10 minutes

Cook Time: 10 minutes

Ingredients:

2 cups water

1 cup steel-cut oats

1 cup almond milk

¼ cup walnuts, chopped

2 tablespoons flaxseeds, ground

2 tablespoons chia seeds

2 bananas, peeled and mashed

1 teaspoon vanilla extract

1 teaspoon cinnamon powder

How To:

1. Add water, oats, almond milk, flaxseed, walnuts, chia seeds, vanilla, bananas, cinnamon to your Instant Pot and

provides it a pleasant toss.

2. Lock the lid and cook on high for 10 minutes.
3. Release the pressure naturally and open the lid.
4. Divide the combination amongst bowls and serve.
5. Enjoy!

Nutrition (Per Serving)

Calories: 200

Fat: 4

Carbohydrates: 11g

Protein: 4g

Traditional Frittata

Serving: 6

Prep Time: 10 minutes

Cook Time: 5 minutes

Ingredients:

2 tablespoons almond milk

Just a pinch pepper

6 eggs, cracked and whisked

2 tablespoons parsley, chopped

1 tablespoon low-fat cheese, shredded

1 cup of water

How To:

1. Take a bowl and add the eggs, almond milk, pepper, cheese, and parsley. Whisk well.

2. Take a pan that might slot in your Instant Pot and grease with cooking spray.

3. Pour the egg mix into the pan.

4. Add a cup of water to your pot and place a steamer basket.

5. Add the pan within the basket.

6. Lock the lid and cook on high for five minutes.

7. Release the pressure naturally over 10 minutes.

8. Remove the lid and divide the frittata amongst serving plates.

9. Enjoy!

Nutrition (Per Serving)

Calories: 200

Fat: 4g

Carbohydrates: 17g

Protein: 6g

Pepperoni Omelet

Serving: 2

Prep Time: 5 minutes

Cook Time: 20 minutes

Ingredients:

3 eggs

7 pepperoni slices

1 teaspoon coconut cream

Salt and freshly ground black pepper, to taste 1 tablespoon butter

How To:

1. Take a bowl and whisk eggs with all the remaining ingredients in it.
2. Then take a skillet and warmth butter.
3. Pour quarter of the egg mixture into your skillet.
4. After that, cook for two minutes per side.
5. Repeat to use the whole batter.

6. Serve warm and enjoy!

Nutrition (Per Serving)

Calories: 141

Fat: 11.5g

Carbohydrates: 0.6g

Protein: 8.9g

Eggy Tomato Scramble

Serving: 2

Prep Time: 10 minutes

Cook Time: 5 minutes

Ingredients:

2 whole eggs

½ cup fresh basil, chopped

2 tablespoons olive oil

½ teaspoon red pepper flakes, crushed

1 cup grape tomatoes, chopped

Salt and pepper to taste

How To:

1. Take a bowl and whisk in eggs, salt, pepper, red pepper flakes and blend well.

2. Add tomatoes, basil, and mix.

3. Take a skillet and place over medium-high heat.

4. Add the egg mixture and cook for five minutes until cooked and scrambled.

5. Enjoy!

Nutrition (Per Serving)

Calories: 130

Fat: 10g

Carbohydrates: 8g

Protein: 1.8g

Breakfast Fruit Pizzas

Ingredients

Two whole-wheat pita flatbreads

7 ounces Arla Original Cream Cheese

1-2 teaspoons honey

1/2 teaspoon pure vanilla extract

Three kiwi skin removed and sliced

1/2 cup sliced strawberries

1/2 cup blackberries

1/4 cup blueberries

Two raspberries for the center

Instructions

1. Preheat the oven to broil. Put the entire wheat pita flatbreads within the oven. Broil for 1 minute and switch over. Broilfor one minute more. you'll also toast the entire pita bread during a kitchen appliance. Set the dough aside to chill.

2. Take a bowl and blend the cheese, honey, and vanilla. Spread the cheese on the pita bread.

3. Decorate the fruit on top of the cheese. dig slices and serve immediately.

4. Note-you can use your favorite fruit. Bananas, peaches, pineapple, oranges, nectarines would even be good!

Peanut Butter Overnight Oats

Ingredients

Oats

Half of cup unsweetened plain almond milk (or sub other dairy-free milk, such as coconut, soy, or hemp!) 3/4 Tbsp of chia seed

2 Tbsp of natural salted peanut butter or almond butter (creamy or crunchy // or sub other nut or seed butter)

1 Tbsp of maple syrup (or sub coconut sugar, natural brown sugar, or stevia to taste) half of cup gluten-loose rolled oats (rolled oats are best, vs. Steel-cut or quick-cooking) Toppings optional

Sliced banana, strawberries, or raspberries Flaxseed meal or additional chia seed Granola

Instructions

1. Take a little bowl with a lid, add almond milk, chia seeds, spread, and syrup (or every other sweetener) and stir with a spoon to mix. The spread doesn't got to be alright blended with the almond milk (doing so leaves swirls of spread to enjoy the next day).

2. Add oats and stir a couple of extra times. Then depress with a spoon to form sure all oats were moistened and areimmersed in almond milk.

3. Cover tightly with a lid or seal and set within the fridge overnight (or for a minimum of 6 hours) to place/soak.

4. the next day, open and knowledge as is or garnish with preferred toppings.

5. Overnight oats will preserve within the refrigerator for 2-three days, though high-quality within the primary 12-24 hours in our experience. Not freezer friendly.

Nutrition

Calories: 452, Fat: 22.8g, Saturated fat: 4.1g, Sodium: 229mgPotassium:479mgCarbohydrates: 51.7g Fiber: 8.3gSugar: 15.8g Protein: 14.6g

Wedge Salad Skewers

Ingredients

One head of iceberg lettuce (cut into wedge pieces)

Four Roma tomatoes cut in half

One red onion (cut into 1-inch pieces)

Two avocados cut into 1-inch pieces

Five slices of bacon cooked and cut into thirds

One cucumber (sliced (peeled or unpeeled))

Eight wooden skewers

Two green onions (diced)

1 5 oz container blue cheese crumbles One bottle blue cheese dressing

Instructions

1. One skewer at a time adds an iceberg wedge, tomato, onion, avocado, two pieces of bacon, every other iceberg wedge, and then cucumber.

2. Continue till all skewers have been made, then garnish with crumbled blue cheese, blue cheese dressing, and diced leafy green onions.

Nutrition

Calories: 238kcal, Fat: 19g, Saturated fat: 6gCholesterol: 25mg Sodium: 401mgPotassium: 573mgCarbohydrates: 10g Fiber: 5g Sugar: 3gProtein: 8gVitamin A: 890%Vitamin C: 13.9%Calcium: 144%Iron: 0.9%

Hearty Chicken Fried Rice

Serving: 4

Prep Time: 10 minutes

Cook Time: 12 minutes

Ingredients:

1 teaspoon olive oil

4 large egg whites

1 onion, chopped

2 garlic cloves, minced

12 ounces skinless chicken breasts, boneless, cut into ½ inch cubes

½ cup carrots, chopped

½ cup frozen green peas

cups long grain brown rice, cooked

tablespoons soy sauce, low sodium

How To:

1. Coat skillet with oil, place it over medium-high heat.
2. Add egg whites and cook until scrambled.
3. Sauté onion, garlic and chicken breasts for six minutes.
4. Add carrots, peas and keep cooking for 3 minutes.
5. Stir in rice, season with soy.
6. Add cooked egg whites, stir for 3 minutes.
7. Enjoy!

Nutrition (Per Serving)

Calories: 353

Fat: 11g

Carbohydrates: 30g

Protein: 23g

Veggie Quesadillas with Cilantro Yogurt Dip

Ingredients

1 cup beans, black or pinto

2 Tablespoons cilantro, chopped

½ bell pepper, finely chopped

½ cup corn kernels

1 cup low-fat shredded cheese

Six soft corn tortillas

One medium carrot, shredded

½ jalapeno pepper, finely minced (optional)

CILANTRO YOGURT DIP

1 cup plain nonfat yogurt

2 Tablespoons cilantro, finely chopped

Juice from ½ of a lime

Instructions

. Preheat large skillet over low heat.

2. Line up three tortillas. Spread cheese, corn, beans, cilantro, shredded carrots, and peppers over the tortillas.

3. Cover all sides with a 2nd tortilla.

4. Place a tortilla on a dry plate and warmth until cheese is melted and tortilla is slightly golden after 3 minutes.

5. Flip and cook another side until golden, about 1 minute.

6. Inside a small bowl, mix the nonfat yogurt, cilantro, and juice.

7. Cut each quesadilla into four wedges (12 wedges total) and serve three wedges per person with about ¼ cup of the dip.

8. Refrigerate leftovers within 2 hours.

Yogurt with Almonds & Honey

Ingredients

Non-fat greek yoghurt-Nonfat, plain-16 oz-453 grams

Almonds-Nuts, raw-1/4 cup, whole-35.8 grams

Honey-2 tsp-14.1 grams

Directions

Rough-chop almonds and blend into yogurt and honey. Enjoy!

Nutrition

Calories 517

Carbs 36g

Fat 20g

Protein 54g

Fiber 5g

Net carbs 31g

Sodium 164mg

Cholesterol 23mg

Quick Buffalo Chicken Salad

Ingredients

Pepper or hot sauce-Ready-to-serve-4 tbsp-57.6 grams

Canned chicken-No broth-1 cup-205 grams

Spinach-Raw-2 cup-60 grams

Tomatoes-Green, raw-Two medium-246 grams

Directions

Mix hot sauce with chicken. Spread spinach and tomatoes on the top. Toss together and enjoy it!

Nutrition

Calorie 456

Carbs 18g

Fat 18g

Protein 57g

Fiber 4g

Net carbs 13g

Sodium 2590mg

Cholesterol 103mg

American Tuna

Ingredients

Tuna-Fish, light, canned in water, drained solids-Two can-330 grams

Light mayonnaise-Salad dressing, light-2 tbsp-30 grams Celery-Cooked, boiled, drained, without a salt-1/4 cup, diced-37.5 grams

Pickles-Cucumber, dill or kosher dill-One large (4" long)-135 grams

Wheat bread-Two slice-50 grams

Directions

1. Mix all ingredients in a bowl.
2. Serve with bread.

Nutrition

Calories 512

Carbs 32g

Fat 12g

Protein 71g

Fiber 4g

Net carbs 28g

Sodium 2443mg

Cholesterol 124mg

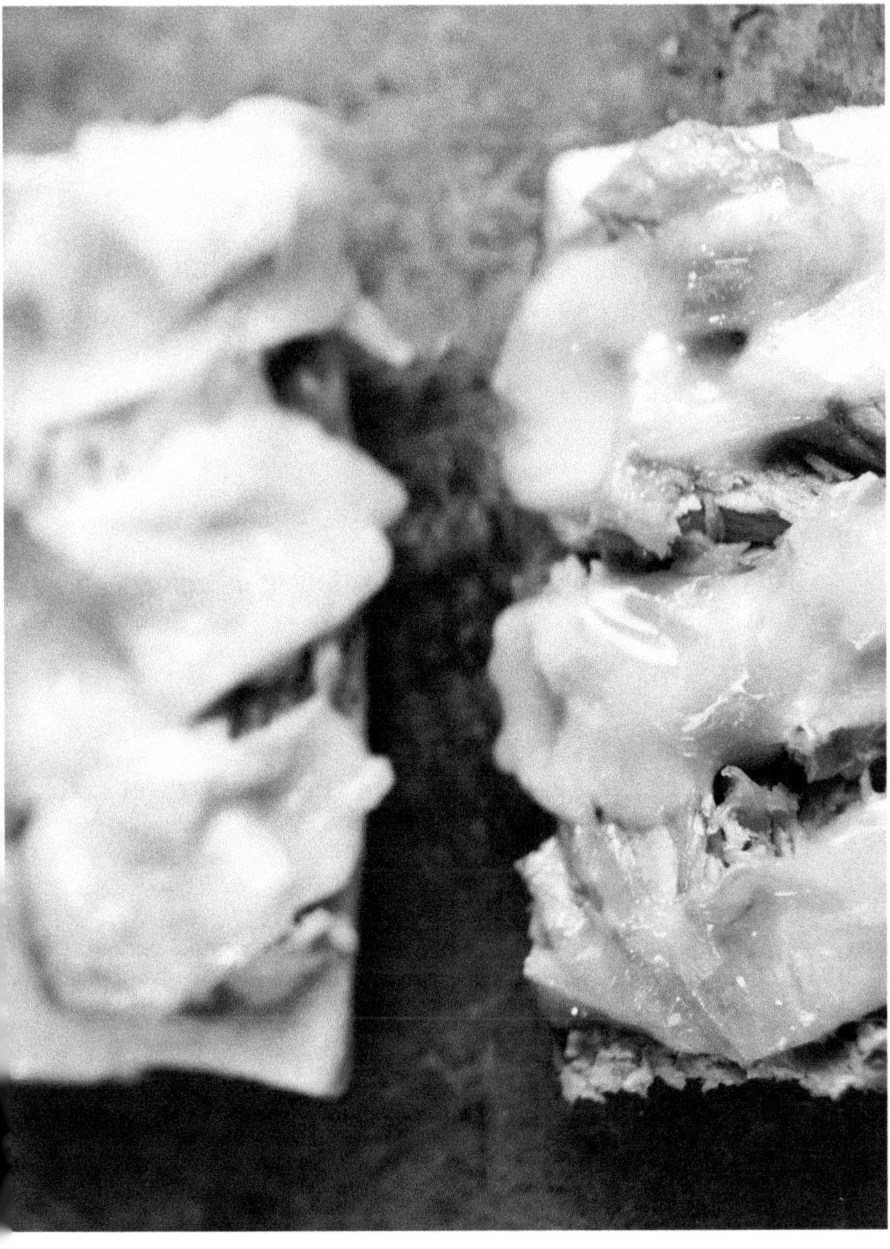

Pimento Cheese Sandwich

Ingredients

Pimento cheese-Pasteurized process-2 oz-56.7 grams Multi-grain bread-Four slices regular-104 grams

Directions

1. Spread the pimento cheese over the bread.
2. Then, a slice of bread to form a sandwich. Enjoy!

Nutrition

Calories 488 Carbs 46g Fat 22g Protein 26g Fiber 8g Net carbs 38g Sodium 915mg Cholesterol 53mg

Hearty Pork Belly Casserole

Serving: 4

Prep Time: 5 minutes

Cook Time: 25 minutes

Ingredients:

8 pork belly slices, cut into small pieces

3 large onions, chopped

4 tablespoons lemon

Juice of 1 lemon

Seasoning as you needed

How To:

1. Take an outsized autoclave and place it over medium heat.

2. Add onions and sweat them for five minutes.

3. Add side of pork slices and cook until the meat browns and onions become golden.

4. Cover with water and add honey, lemon peel, sunflower seeds, pepper, and shut the pressure seal.

5. Pressure cook for 40 minutes.

6. Serve and luxuriate in with a garnish of fresh chopped parsley if you favor.

Nutrition (Per Serving)

Calories: 753

Fat: 41g

Carbohydrates: 68g

Protein: 30g

Apple Pie Crackers

Serving: 100 crackers

Prep Time: 10 minutes

Cooking Time: 120 minutes

Ingredients:

2 tablespoons + 2 teaspoons avocado oil

1 medium Granny Smith apple, roughly chopped ¼ cup Erythritol

1/4 cup sunflower seeds, ground

1 ¾ cups roughly ground flax seeds

./8 teaspoon Ground cloves

/8 teaspoon ground cardamom

; tablespoons nutmeg

¼ teaspoon ground ginger

Iow To:

Pre-heat your oven to 225 degrees F.

. Line two baking sheets with parchment paper and keep

them on the side.

3. Add oil, apple, Erythritol to a bowl and blend.

4. Transfer to kitchen appliance and add remaining ingredients, process until combined.

5. Transfer batter to baking sheets, spread evenly and dig crackers.

6. Bake for 1 hour, flip and bake for an additional hour.

7. allow them to cool and serve.

8. Enjoy!

Nutrition (Per Serving)

Total Carbs: 0.9g (%)

Fiber: 0.5g

Protein: 0.4g (%)

Fat: 2.1g (%)

Paprika Lamb Chops

Serving: 4

Prep Time: 10 minutes

Cook Time: 15 minutes

Ingredients:

1 lamb rack, cut into chops pepper to taste 1 tablespoon paprika

1/2 cup cumin powder

1/2 teaspoon chili powder

How To:

1. Take a bowl and add paprika, cumin, chili, pepper, and stir.

2. Add lamb chops and rub the mixture.

3. Heat grill over medium-temperature and add lamb chops, cook for five minutes.

4. Flip and cook for five minutes more, flip again.

5. Cook for two minutes, flip and cook for two minutes more.

6. Serve and enjoy!

Nutrition (Per Serving)

Calories: 200

Fat: 5g

Carbohydrates: 4g

Protein: 8g

Chicken & Goat Cheese Skillet

Ingredients

1/2 pound of boneless skinless chicken breasts, cut into 1-inch pieces

1/4 teaspoon salt

1/8 teaspoon pepper

Two teaspoons olive oil

1 cup sliced fresh asparagus (1-inch pieces)

One garlic clove, minced

Three plum tomatoes, chopped

Three tablespoons 2% milk

Two tablespoons herbed fresh goat cheese, crumbled Hot cooked rice or pasta

Additional goat cheese, optional

Directions

1. Toss chicken with salt and pepper. Heat oil at medium heat; saute chicken until not pink, 4-6 minutes.Remove from pan; keep warm.

2. Add asparagus to skillet; cook and blend at medium-high

heat 1 minute. Add garlic; cook and stir 30 seconds. Stirin tomatoes, milk, and two tablespoons cheese; cook, covered, over medium heat until cheese begins to melt, 2-3 minutes. Stir in chicken. Serve with rice. If desired, top with additional cheese.

Nutrition

251 calories, 11g fat, 74mg cholesterol, 447mg sodium, 8g carbohydrate (5g sugars, 3g fiber), 29g protein. Diabetic Exchanges: 4 lean meat, two fat, one vegetable.

Green Curry Salmon with Green Beans

Ingredients

Four salmon fillets (4 ounces each)

1 cup light coconut milk

Two tablespoons green curry paste

1 cup uncooked instant brown rice

1 cup reduced-sodium chicken broth

1/8 teaspoon pepper

3/4-pound fresh green beans, trimmed

One teaspoon sesame oil

One teaspoon sesame seeds, toasted

Lime wedges

Directions

Preheat oven to 400°. Place salmon in an 8-in. Square baking dish. Mix together coconut milk and curry paste; pour over salmon. Bake, uncovered, till fish simply starts offevolved to flake effortlessly with a fork, 15-20 minutes.

2. Meanwhile, during a small saucepan, integrate rice, broth and pepper; convey to a boil. Reduce warmth; simmer, covered, 5 minutes. Remove from heat; let stand five minutes.

3. In a big saucepan, area steamer basket over 1 in. Of water. Place inexperienced beans inside the basket; convey water to a boil. Reduce heat to take care of a simmer; steam, covered, till beans are crisp-tender, 7-10 minutes. Toss with vegetable oil and sesame seeds.

4. Serve salmon with rice, beans and lime wedges. Spoon coconut sauce over the salmon.

Nutrition Facts

366 calories, 17g fat (5g saturated fat), 57mg cholesterol, 340mg sodium, 29g carbohydrate (5g sugars, 4g fibre), 24g protein.

Greek Salad

Serving: 4

Prep Time: 6 minutes

Cook Time: Nil

Ingredients:

2 cucumbers, diced

2 tomatoes, sliced

1 green lettuce, cut into thin strips

2 red bell peppers, cut

½ cup black olives pitted

3 ½ ounces feta cheese, cut

1 red onion, sliced

2 tablespoons olive oil

2 tablespoons lemon juice

Sunflower seeds and pepper to taste

Direction

1. Dice cucumbers and slice up the tomatoes.

2. Tear the lettuce and cut it into thin strips.

3. De-seed and cut the peppers into strips.

4. Take a salad bowl and mix in all the listed vegetables, add olives and feta cheese (cut into cubes).

5. Take a small cup and mix in olive oil and lemon juice, season with sunflower seeds and pepper.

6. Pour mixture into the salad and toss well, enjoy!

Nutrition (Per Serving)

Calories: 132

Fat: 4g

Carbohydrates: 3g

Protein: 5g

Fancy Greek Orzo Salad

Serving: 4

Prep Time: 5 minutes and 24 hours chill time

Cook Time: 10 minutes

Ingredients:

1 cup orzo pasta, uncooked

½ cup fresh parsley, minced

6 teaspoons olive oil

1 onion, chopped

1 ½ teaspoons oregano

How To:

1. Cook the orzo and drain them.
2. Add to a serving dish.
3. Add 2 teaspoons of oil.
4. Take another dish and add parsley, onion, remaining oil and oregano.

5. Season with sunflower seeds, pepper according to your taste.

6. Pour the mixture over the orzo and let it chill for 24 hours.

7. Serve and enjoy at lunch!

Nutrition (Per Serving)

Calories: 399

Fat: 12g

Carbohydrates: 55g

Protein:16g

Homely Tuscan Tuna Salad

Serving: 4

Prep Time: 5-10 minutes

Cook Time: Nil

Ingredients:

15 ounces small white beans

6 ounces drained chunks of light tuna

cherry tomatoes, quartered

4 scallions, trimmed and sliced

2 tablespoons lemon juice

How To:

Add all of the listed ingredients to a bowl and gently stir.

Season with sunflower seeds and pepper accordingly, enjoy!

Nutrition (Per Serving)

Calories: 322

Fat: 8g

Carbohydrates: 32g

Protein:30g

Asparagus Loaded Lobster Salad

Serving: 4

Prep Time: 10 minutes

Cook Time: Nil

Ingredients:

8 ounces lobster, cooked and chopped

3 ½ cups asparagus, chopped and steamed

2 tablespoons lemon juice

4 teaspoons extra virgin olive oil

¼ teaspoon kosher sunflower seeds

Pepper

½ cup cherry tomatoes halved

1 basil leaf, chopped

2 tablespoons red onion, diced

How To:

1. Whisk in lemon juice, sunflower seeds, pepper in a bowl and mix with oil.

2. Take a bowl and add the rest of the ingredients.

3. Toss well and pour dressing on top.

Serve and enjoy!

Nutrition (Per Serving)

Calories: 247

Fat: 10g

Carbohydrates: 14g

Protein: 27g

Tasty Yogurt and Cucumber Salad

Serving: 4

Prep Time: 10 minutes

Cook Time: Nil

Ingredients:

5-6 small cucumbers, peeled and diced

1 (8 ounces) container plain Greek yogurt

2 garlic cloves, minced

1 tablespoon fresh mint, minced

Sea sunflower seeds and fresh black pepper

How To:

Take a large bowl and add cucumbers, garlic, yogurt, mint.

Season with sunflower seeds and pepper.

Refrigerate the salad for 1 hour and serve.

Enjoy!

Nutrition (Per Serving)

Calories: 74

Fat: 0.7g

Carbohydrates: 16g

Protein: 2g

Unique Eggplant Salad

Serving: 3

Prep Time: 10 minutes

Cook Time: 30 minutes

Ingredients:

2 eggplants, peeled and sliced

2 garlic cloves

2 green bell pepper, sliced, seeds removed ½ cup fresh parsley

½ cup mayonnaise, low fat, low sodium Sunflower seeds and black pepper

How To:

1. Preheat your oven to 480 degrees F.

2. Take a baking pan and add eggplant, bell peppers and season with black [MOU15][F16]pepper to it.

3. Bake for about 30 minutes.

4. Flip the vegetables after 20 minutes.

5. Then, take a bowl, add baked vegetables and all the

remaining ingredients.

6. Mix well.

7. Serve and enjoy!

Nutrition (Per Serving)

Calories: 196

Fat: 108.g

Carbohydrates: 13.4g

Protein: 14.6g

Zucchini Pesto Salad

Serving: 4

Prep Time: 10 minutes

Cook Time: 10 minutes

Ingredients:

2 cups spiral pasta

2 zucchini, sliced and halved

4 tomatoes, cut

1 cup white mushrooms, cut

1 small red onion, chopped

2 tablespoons fresh basil leaves, chopped

2 tablespoons sunflower oil

1 tablespoon lemon juice

Pepper and sunflower seeds to taste

How To:

1. Cook the pasta according to the package instructions, drain and rinse under cold water.

2. Take a large bowl and add zucchini, tomatoes, mushrooms, onion, and pasta.

3. Mix well,

4. In a food processor, add oil, lemon juice, basil, blue cheese, black, and process well.

5. Pour the mixture over the salad and toss well.

6. Serve and enjoy!

Nutrition (Per Serving)

Calories: 301

Fat: 25g

Net Carbohydrates: 7g

Protein: 10g

Lightning Source UK Ltd.
Milton Keynes UK
UKHW020816250521
384336UK00004B/138

9 781802 773958